MW00887430

Tips On Throwing
A Housewarming Party
In A Small Space

Moors Poetry Collective
Nantucket, MA.

DEDICATION

This book is dedicated to the daily search for the right words.

CONTENTS

Acknowledgments   i

Andrew Bauld   1

Neil Brosnan   7

Kathy Butterworth   14

Len Germinara   19

Amy Jenness   23

Kimberly Nolan   30

John Stanton   36

Portraits   43

ANDREW BAULD

The New Age of Exploration

The map tells us
only half of what
we need to know
because there is no
conversion
from miles to longing.

Erase
the Prime Meridian
and the Equator.
Instead, draw me the intersection of
the day I left
flowers in your mailbox
and the night I threw
the ladder off the porch.

A better cartographer must be able
to triangulate
those invisible distances,
to model this reality
and label some of the dragons.

Radio Time Travel

love between stations

memory hues
wedded to sound

notes of plum purple blue
rebuilding worn away places
revising history

charcoal gray strays
leaving you
to your own devices

sea glass green
reminder of a room
as it might have been

black obsidian
singing then now and the next time
whenever that may be

revolving into
blinding yellow orange
only seen from the side

with a breeze through the open window
reds that warm the inside out
and her ponytail swish

Blue Hour

The contents of a thirty rack
littered by the side of the road
the empties scattered near the woods
like pick-up-sticks

they picked us up all night long
flooding our limbs with firefly
incandescence
buzzing through fingers and toes
jumpstarting our hearts
beyond buzzed

beats measured in kilowatts
into the early morning vagabond
hours when the world loses
all pretense of ownership
you perched on an outcropping
shining
from your teeth and your eyes
some gorgeous
living lighthouse

attracting those
blue hour phantoms
invisible unknowns
except for their staccato entreaties
detached from the darkness
for a spare drink or something more effective
we held court with the shadows
until they too faded

3

then
when we were the only ones left awake
the water
linoleum cool on our blistering feet
we doggy-paddled with the last two beer bottles
clamped between our teeth
tethered at the edge
alone
sure we could hold
on to this moment forever

St. Brendan's Island

The Irish monk spoke of
a paradise
he had visited
only once before.
Somewhere
lonely in the Atlantic
the sun never sets
and the rivers run with fresh water.
The trees bare heavy fruit
and the birds sing sweet.

I.

Let's get into the bathtub,
you and I,
pack it with all the things we'll need:
a flashlight, a radio, a few favorite books,
a deck of cards, a razor that my face and your legs can share,
and we'll bring some of that homemade granola you made
that morning we skipped work because of the snow.
I came in from the driveway after shoveling a path
to a warm hallway with a smell that reminded me of
Thanksgiving morning.

II.

We drifted along the wide waters
for three years and eleven months

when finally we hit solid land.
You went off, tattered dressed and quiet,
into the woods beyond the beach.
I must have fallen asleep, still curled up
in the bath, surrounded by a few
rain soaked playing cards
and the discarded bones of fish
we had caught along the way.
I think I called out your name once or twice
in the night.

III.

It was in the middle of all things,
after burying the dog,
that I returned to find the tub
readied to set sail. They must have fitted it out
when I wasn't looking.
The sail was freshly patched
with fragments of a dress,
a torn leg from a pair of jeans.
The nose pointed west.
I cut the line and let the current
take me where it would,
toward the yellowing afternoon.

NEIL BROSNAN

the revolutionist

hunted down
they found him in an open field
riddled with scraps of poetry
half thought out verse
set in awkward measure

broken mouth
dammed with thwarted doves
fingers crushed
stained with bitter ink-fret
one upturned palm caked with blood
the body's final prayer
sensate oblation

at last at peace
splayed across
gaunt furrows of barren asylum...

out of his heart's conclusion

a single stalk of wheat.

my heart man

beatman, beatman, beatman
Duluoz, Kerouac...
Lowell son, Columbia son,
Denver, Frisco, Mexico son.

Tokay tippler, type a page of words
a minute man. Run on
Jack-mouth unpunctuated bhikku con-
man, road man, dharma man, subterranean.

Juiced on benzedrine
Lucky Strikes and blood red
any-port-in-a-storm-man.
Whose madcap haiku life ended
shy of its seventeenth syllable.
Whose strange blue collar
synthesis of corkscrew zen
bottled in alcoholic catholicism
made me hobo drunk-man, witlessly wise
hung over on six page sentences
riffing improvisational Buddha, hepcat Jesus
skid row bums and the ever lurking void voice.
While he staggared on

grinning shitfaced and unshaven
losing his tao-way across
Americas middle stretch,
mid life crisis; until he succumbed, man
and was undone.

I hear you still, Duluoz
in jazz verse carry you
pulsing in my heart,
my heart, my heart,
my heart...
my heart man.

hobo wood

                    a cluster of pines
huddled on a Polpis hill
stands like hobos would
if they were still allowed to gather

stooped over forlorn needles
nodding into wind
with gaping smiles
aching limbs
nostalgic for those days gone by
when Forest
was the only language spoken.

blue ribbons

the lady in question
elbow deep in organic broccoli
with rubber flip flops on
had a tattooed tick
wandering across the top of each fat foot
swollen from the weight of generous hips
wrapped in an orange mu-mu
I couldn't miss
as I tried to roll my grocery cart past
in search of long green beans
avocado and tofu.

but the aisle would not contain the two of us
so I waited and watched
beads of sweat collect beneath
the bulb of her little pug nose
to wet the edge of her protruding tongue
clenched between a disaster of teeth
as her hands dug deeper
frantic for I could only imagine
the perfect floret
she could down with a slab
of two inch thick sirloin
mashed potatoes, summer squash
yams, cresent buns and
from the looks of her
a six-pack of Pabst Blue Ribbon

the beer that made Milwaukee famous.

another cat
(Franz Wright)

the heels of his poor man shoes
were each worn down
on the outside edge
and the laces were white string
knotted to where the black had broken...
he looked ill at ease
a shabby catastrophe
dismantled and put back together
way too many times
shy and uncomfortable
in a weird
slouched
off kilter kind of way

but the words he coaxed
when he finally read
strained through some dark reserve
intoned their way up out of his throat
and filled the room with music
erasing any sense of what
he was not
and as I listened
I swear he disappeared

and another cat
completely beyond description
          took his place.

Venice

your cool blue
spreads out
unspools laid back
along conformity's edge
West Coast hip
transcendental

hash smoke in the sea breeze
sidewalk art work
music
bohemian vibes
graffiti dharma
surf and skate board
troubadours
rightiously zen bent

street kids, tourists, tofu hippies
Muscle Beach
pulse specific Pacific poetry
voodoo yoga
all posture and trance
karmic attude
beatific bliss

funky pastiche of
sunblock, sweat, incense, patchouli
rising in a haze of OM
above the beautiful madness
man

all these radiant heads

KATHY BUTTERWORTH

Artist Who Paints Skies
inspired by S Heaney's *Artist*

I think about his loneliness
his inability to leave the path, his firmness
of feet in a mucky landscape.

The way he guards the beach mornings
when no one is there to be guarded
And his ridiculous hats and shirts
to show he knows he's laughed at by many
and by himself and stands at ease with that.
Digging into skies like a miner
in a town where no one mines.
The years passing and him riding them out
holding on loose and steady.
His eyes alive studying each new day's infant sky.
He in direct conversation with sky.

For Kevin Powers who wrote The Yellow Birds

True
I am not in Iraq
blowing bullets into an old woman
nor am I her granddaughter
hunched in the shadow of a building
I lean back in a soft chair
close to the fire
shifting burden

What you don't know,
soldiers come home
tossing in your beds,
    you are not carrying the weight alone
    Yes, it is personal
    you signed up
    maybe thought you could prove something
while I slipped into my own easy life

What you don't know
is another haunting
scours the ones that let you go

So what,
I fall into an easy sleep
rest well
while you slog through a line of bottles
until darkness takes over

Here's what,
I let you carry my burden
and can't make that up
sending money to soldier funds

Hitch-hiker

the driver maybe 30
turned onto a gravelly pull-off
unseen from the road

and tried to slide her
across the seat of his black truck

the cab had one of those
crammed backs
where a young boy sat

What's the matter?
he asked her
in front of the dark eyed child
I have to go she said
pulling up her knapsack
feeling for the door handle

You don't believe in love?

her eyes caught the boy's pool eyes

C'mon he coaxed
she twisted free
jumped down

You're not getting back in he said
It's gonna be dark in 5 minutes
and you don't have a ride

she swung the door shut
walked away
chills like fire up her neck
 on the road she could feel him
he could do anything
he had his son in the truck
traffic had thinned
still twenty miles to make
and the sound of a car behind

Him
   small son in the front

she looked away
felt him pass

he could do anything
he had his son in the truck

The Sky Waits for No One

As he lifts the brush
the sky lowers the curtain
leaving that same muted tone
only an artist would deconstruct

but he dug for color yesterday
and a hundred days before
and face it
half his skies whiten canvases

piled in corners of the studio
(nobody buys white skies
looming over slate waters
reminding them of doomed vacations)

maybe he should stop
this obsession with the vast
  hone in on an apple
(a whim without air he knows)

he has to burn through skies
until there's nothing left
to understand
he's a painter of skies, that's all

LEN GERMINARA

I Believe in Circular Rotation

The snow comes, a mute swan to cover my feet
Of grey clay
To be rendered down when the weather warms
A puddle's indentations
Briefest mention in a drought
Sing my day's diminution a Beatles tune
Day tripper in a Somerset South Sea story
Dance for a sixpence
Without pants
Ignore the ignominious
As they you
Tip your hat a swell in the deep end
Hold your nose against the din and
All that that entails
Entrails and garden paths lead you astray
Wink of a ponytail
Swishing hey how you doing
It warms

Midafternoon light flickers on
Reflective surfaces distorts all images
Real or imagined in sleep's recesses
A nap most welcome
Settle for a quick smoke
Turn off the cell phone unplug the computer
Yank
Throw the modem over your shoulder for good luck
Hang your socks over the radiator
Slip on a disc
Play some NOLA Gris-Gris
Tom Tom and Tambourines
Leave your hat on the turntable spinning

Originally appeared in
Of Course, I Could Be Wrong (2014) Nantucket Field Station Press

Pond without a name

Winter-gone bittern
Wades in to last year's
Cattail remnants
Famished isosceles triangle
In search of a meal
That won't catch in her craw

She doesn't see me coming

Until the camera gives me away
Tiny motors and moving pieces
My shaky hands

Startled
She strikes a pose
Nose straight up in the air
Like sedges ready to scatter seed

Ragged as an old mill saw
Hung on a barn wall

I move closer
She's broken glass
Moving her air frame
Into the wind

One more pose

Before she goes
On with her morning
Somewhere else

Originally appeared in
Of Course, I Could Be Wrong (2014) Nantucket Field Station Press

Bourbon Street Tomorrow

We boarded the train
in the dark
Cold dragon's breath
Mid-winter vortex

Boston to NOLA
Holes in our
Spanish leather

Sleet raking us
On the long walk
To our sleeper car

Where
Thankfully our
Beds are already turned down

This is a work in progress
We'll need our rest

A day and a half by train
Just the ticket

The fading shadows applause
Reflecting on the window pane
In Pennsylvania

Everything else falls away
to the end of the line
Where Jazz and Oysters
Await us

Originally appeared in
Of Course, I Could Be Wrong (2014) Nantucket Field Station Press

AMY JENNESS

Winter Bird

Black crow, black crow
dark days
head bent low
glass shard flash
blue paper scrap
your mate has gone
leaving you
to pick the yard
alone.
They lived in the
blue-black pick-up
parked by the road
reading the paper
passing time
napping
cat stretched happily
along the black dash
basking in the
sun's stored warmth

Every day he drove her
to the store
to work
She picks up
shiny receipts
blown from paper
sacks
cigarette butts,
dusty coins

He waited in the truck
she cleaned the
parking lot
crawling under cars
clearing out the
windblown scraps
trapped against the curb
and long forgotten

An old married couple
in their day
moving slow
intent on
collecting the
carelessly
unwanted
bits
the worthless
leftovers
that surround us

As each truck bed filled
with scraps and bits
it was parked in
their yard.
He found another
old tired truck.
They continue
to collect
He the chauffeur
she busy bent over
a squirrel
a crow
He died last year
Driverless now
she cleans along
the road
by her house,
between the
abandoned trucks
Bent over
spider-veined
hands caress
frozen grass
solitary
dressed in black
long white hair
sweeping the ground

Island Republic of Wind

The sandpiper tips and rides the wind
sideways
brown boomerang falling
down,
elegantly down
to the dark sea.

The wires whistle, taut and blown
sideways.
Invisible air saws a three string
violin
that throat sings
a ghoulish zombie moan

The sleek yacht rolls, knife-edged ride
sideways
through chops of green marbled
ocean
White sheets and metal cleats
harness a wilderness of sky and wind.

The flags unfurl, rippled and pulled
sideways.
Up high, a sign to passersby.
This is home
we are citizens of the
island republic of wind.

Friday Night

The men's hockey team won
and went on a bender

Penned together in
a big white bus
they idled
in the liquor store alley

         waiting
Avoiding
someone's boss
someone's sister-in-law

Waiting
for their hip flasks
to be filled
their fat, stinking
rolled Cuban gold

Canine mutts
old and young

We won
it's party time
at the
Sea Dog
House of Ale

The bus rolled out
into the night
flying on a sonic carpet
of war whoops
pounding fists
          that rattled the glass

One player spotted me
and suggested
we get married

the bus pulled away
and headed for town

Eagle Prayer

I ask the wild bird
to deliver my dreams

he agrees

open winged
tipped forward
lifted to the sky
for a moment
intent
and then
movement

he flies

he has the list
in his claw

       desire
       fear
       hope
       love

on his way to
give it to god

Big black bird
ferocious ancient king
thank you for
taking these small
human things.

29

KIMBERLY NOLAN

41 years

tonight you said
there was one star
at the tip of the crescent moon

you said they were close together
  an odd pair
  yet a perfect match

after you left
I looked out the small barn window
above the last stall

the moon and lone star
were so far apart
an entire fallow field
stretched between them

end of spring

we speak of watermelon seeds
lettuce plugs
onion starts
I tell you the yellow iris bloomed before anything else

you want me to tell you the soil here is wrong
too rocky
too sandy
that nothing can grow in the salt air
that I'm coming home

back east

I try on towns like shoes, she said
mackerel-sky eyes, lines traversing ruddy face
like America's blue highways
no sign of civilization
in her working hands
cigarette smoke circled her cattle dog
unflinching
she talked about ranching
with a defined accent

I pretended to not know
that she drove bucking bulls
to and from Oklahoma
that she had a kid
at 17
that she could pound posts
for a country mile
that he paid for her pickup truck
overflowing with straw bales

that he still loved her

onstage she laughed while she said
I don't play other people's songs
she sang
"Angel From Montgomery"
like it was hers

Tuesday

the palm
of tanned-hide hands
swallows the chicken's head
he pulls

a quick unzip, vertebrae from skull
something snapping, something grinding
something juicing
all at once

I've seen it before
pierce of a paring knife
short slit
the final twitch before stillness
bleeding into a puddle
coagulation
the dog trying to lick it

scalding tank
automatic plucker
heads and feet cut off
necks saved for soup
trachea wrapped around index finger for a good tug

evisceration table
hand sliding in past wrist bone
warm intestines thud into bucket
careful not to break the liver
easiest to find the lungs
by dragging fingernails across ribs

when he pulled I must've winced
he threw her into an old grain bag

stepped close to me
blew a hot, short breath into my eye
like the final candle on a birthday cake
and laughed

going home

heat too heavy to move
the Kousa dogwood leaves
driftwood holds windows open
shades half-drawn
bedroom door too swollen to shut

stickers of saints
peel off pious candles
green for St. Jude
red for St. Francis
white for the Blessed Mother

three blocks away
baseballs ding
off little league bats

the Mente and Collins boys
debate goals, penalties
and out of bounds

skates and sticks
scrape pavement

street lights come on
the neighbor perfects her fiddle
a caged beagle whimpers

the strawberry moon rises
before the late train pulls in

JOHN STANTON

Where is the Bonus Baby Now?

Later, I heard
he drove a cab
in Portsmouth, New Hampshire,
napped sometimes
parked at the curb outside
a local bar, where
the drunks waited
to ride
 in his lefty wisdom
 through the 2 a.m. quiet
dispatcher asleep
 totemic baseball
rolling
under his seat.

The memory braille of
red stitches
conjured cool flashes
that once ran
up his storied
left arm into
the right side of his
brain.

Behind closed lids
he endlessly
toed the rubber
believed the casual arced path
to be one last foolish spring
breeze
until
suddenly
jerked awake
 into cold autumn
finality
by the shadow of
the wall,
and Tony Perez.

"Where is the Bonus Baby Now" appeared in *Aethlon: The Journal of Sport Literature*, (September 2011) under the title "Leephus."

Moonshine And Jesus (West Virginia, 1987)

Faith
and the snakes
to prove it
poured out of them
like tongues of
sacred fire
Stratocaster fueled
biblical certainty
voices of redemption
in the holler.

She loved the fire
the promise of venom
in the engine grit
under his fingernails
as they drifted over her
skin in the shadows
while they raced
past coal tipples
guardrail rumors
slag pile
brimstone
on mountain roads
known only to mountain people

Later
after she spoke
in tongues
secretly to him
tasted moonshine
burn on his lips
she saw
that what they
said
about the Holy Ghost
might be
true.

Taking Stock

second bicuspid
lost in 1978
never to return
same as my virginity
gone so long I cannot remember
who with
no
I remember
fondly
except afterwards
she flipped on the t.v.
while I walked onto
the motel balcony
decided against calling her
outside
to look
at the stars.

meniscus tear
cartilage memory
rumor of a limp
a comma stitched
and whitening
we grow into our pain
until it becomes
a postcard
from someplace
we cannot remember
a snore
on the other side
of the bed
we cannot sleep
without.

Travelogue

Guatemalan Weekend

feral dogs packed
into a Friday morning van
while the lion awaits breakfast

we hold hands
on the Saturday night
midway

carnival barkers
games of chance
paint huffers and glue sniffers

their vacant Sunday morning
eyes reflect calliope light
while the lion sleeps

A Private Home in Cork

we lie about marriage
lie awake in that naked

bed as Jesus opens
his robe to show us

his sacred bleeding heart
let the bastards try something now

he says to himself washing
dishes downstairs.

Home, Sunday Afternoon

three past ripe berries
in a thorny embrace

you close your eyes
sit in moments of sunlight

I begin to say something
until I hear your breath.

Back in the Old Neighborhood

his dead wife always fed
the winter birds

while he ate August supper
bare-chested and remembered the lion.

PORTRAITS

Portrait of the Dead, Unknown

By Andrew Bauld

He labors everyday
peddling his blue rusty bike
to and from town,
down and back up the hill.
Must be pushing eighty.

Always looks the same:
tan polo taut from a heavy gut,
pair of white shorts, high white socks.
Stringy legs that move so slow,
barely turning,
somehow keep him upright.
Rainy days he dons a clear plastic poncho.
Even Sisyphus can't stand to be wet.

Head down, no helmet to cover his shock of white hair,
spine curved over the handlebars,
two bent and rusted things.
A quiet breeze should tumble them over.

I haven't seen him in several days.
When I ask neighbors,
The Bike Rider, have you seen him?
they sigh and smile in dim recognition,
say, not in a while.

I find his obituary in the paper
and finally read his name.
No mention of the bike
left leaning against a tree.

gypsy pilgrimage

By Neil Brosnan

Ellen McIlwaine
just burned a hole in my pick-up's radio
WACK could not contain her
could not keep her flames
from filling my cab with smoke.

She got acoustic fire
mojo knuckle, Kottke fret hand
Hendrix dementia
run through fingers
calloused to hum
hoochie-coochie delta
rock and roll dominion
in the ruined cab where screaming pores
sweat out highway bone-smoke
pulled from burning herb
raw as the naugahyde blisters
rising off the roach tarred seat
leaving me
so stoned, I say, red lights be damned
and the rearview mirror dice
kicking up like they were craps again
agree
fire's the name of this epiphany
tongued in aurora borealis octaves
pulsing over undulating fields of incandescent wheat
St. Christopher on the dashboard magnet
and I in a trance race frantic through
till he's burned down

to his iconic sanctified plastic feet
wholly consumed
and it's just as well

cause he ain't allowed to where we're goin.

Hellbent to the crossroad's
in an orange halo of flame
me on a gypsy pilgrimage

with Ellen McIlwain.

Women on the Dunes

By Kathy Butterworth

One cross-legged
sits higher up
jeans taut at knees
a line drawing

one dark haired
clear faced, jowly
sits lower down
round

They speak loudly
against the rushing sound
neither moves closer
to the other

Meanwhile the sea
sparks thousands of times
the sky blues the water
day grows
earth tugs on heat
holds it close

Spring rolls in like a wave
washing the women to silence
which seems to say
they see it coming

Brautigan

By Len Germinara

Richard and I went fishing Monday.
We stopped at Willard's Market,
for smokes, worms, and some Kool-Aid.

Richard had offered to pay.
As usual, Richard only had Monopoly money
little scraps of paper with hand drawn fish
So I gave the attendant $4.00 for a $3.99 purchase.

Worms, we couldn't afford
so we used Kool-Aid,
sat lazy fishing at our river
for the better part of an afternoon.
Toes in the mud,
fish beginning to rise.

I've known Richard for years,
but to be his lover is completely awesome with a capital A,
mouth open,
eyes squeezed tight.
Ah.....

Richard once compared lazy fishing
to loading mercury with a pitchfork.
He often tells me in the afterglow,
breath short,
eyes wide, I see the heavy water rise and I'm gone.

We fish at the North River,
right next to the old mill.
You know the place.
We set about our task
the Kool-Aid slides on the hook smooth.
Everything seems suspended in watermelon sugar.

We didn't catch a fish that day.

I don't know why Richard calls me Trout.
My name is Amy.
He just started calling me Trout one day when we was fishing
And it just stuck.

We was on vacation.
Lake Winnipesaukee, I think.
It was fall and I felt like a rainbow,
now Trout's my name.

Richard used to be famous
to hear him tell it.

It was before I met him.
He said he was considered a humorist.
Funny, nothing he's ever said or done has struck me as funny.

He owns a black cat.
Richard calls him Dogfood.
He often gives the cat's name as an example of his humor.
If you ask me, that ain't funny.
I think it's kind of sad.
I think Richard's sad,
but I love him.

He makes me feel weak and alive all at once.
I don't much understand him,

my education is lacking and he's an educated man.

He never makes me feel lacking though,
And I can almost see the stars as he sees them
in the sound of his voice.

Maybe I'm too casual.
One last remnant of the summer of love.
Long, straight hair.
Bell bottom jeans, Frye boots.
The day we met I said
Richard, I hide the keys to my apartment under the doormat
let yourself in.
I sleep heavy.

He showed up that night like a sombrero that fell from the sky.
Afterward, we lay as crumpled as the linen under us.
Just like that.
I remember thinking, what the hell happened?
It's always like that with Richard,
maybe not quite as hot,
but better than a slap on the ass.

That was the first time he ever slapped me on the ass.
I like it when he does it,
even when I pretend not to like it.
Believe me, I can pretend good.

I told Richard, "I see stars in your voice."
he looked at me like he saw fire for the first time,
but he stayed rooted.
He didn't run.
Richard's not a running man,
at least not the Richard I know,
knew.......

There is never enough time for fishing,
even if fishing is all you have to do.
Fame is a clever trick much like the wonder of a photograph.
I have a photograph of Richard and me.

We set up a camera on a log by our favorite spot.
Fell into focus wrapped in each other's arms.
The timer whirred,
and snapped our shot.

Richard said "Trout,
I love it here with you,
remember that whenever you look at this picture."

The picture of Richard and me hangs in my parlor,
right next to Richard's empty gun rack.

Winner 2003 Cambridge Poetry Award - Best Narrative Poem

Biography of a Stranger

By Amy Jenness

when I first saw you
what surprised me most
was your eyebrows

They connect together,
one crooked horizontal stripe
on a sharply vertical face

A disconcerting line where
there's usually space
Your war-paint eyebrows

your wedge of a nose
spear tip thrust up
made me think you are
of French descent.

A dark skinned southerner
restless carnelian blood
stomping gypsy dancer
Napoleon island tyrant
    --   but Napoleon in the good way

With unannounced
ambitions, an explorer
who trespasses

Who takes or leaves
but mostly just hopes
to see unmapped territory

How do I know all this
based on one glance?
I know because I too

descend down from
combative Normans
with shield and lance

With eyebrows that tell
the tale. And I know
how to read them

Quick Break

By Caitlin Kelley

Brick finished counting out carpaccio in the back kitchen. Oil soaked the skin above his gloves and the hairs on his forearms were flecked with pepper flung from pounding. He pulled at latex fingers with disgust.

Hands rinsed, but still greasy, he pushed out the swinging back door and reached for matches stashed in deep pockets.

The long alley behind the kitchen opened out to the back of the bandstand tent, to the corner of the stage, the guitarist's white pant leg shifting in 4/4 time, and the edges of that mingling, fancy-dressed crowd.

Brick struck sulphur and settled behind a stack of crates, felt drops of sweat dart down his back.

> He remembered a time in New York
> when it was hot like this.
>
> (The humidity must break to rain soon.)
> He'd been washed over by nylon notes then
> too, leaning on elbows that weren't yet
> pan-scorched, in a hat that made him feel
> like peacocking, and he had.

On third drag he peered through plastic grate like a church window and caught a snatch of bright violet. He craned his neck for a full view.

The dress was flowy-light, touched to the ground, exposed the lady's tan shoulders.

Facing the band she backed herself down the alley gravel, until none from the tent could see.

Arms swinging, she began to sway. Her spine moving in little s-curves, in bigger ones, when the beat quickened

A full spin and her dress bloomed like a silk parachute.

Brick remembered a girl from South Slope. He sighed, "hot blood," and realized he was smoking the filter.

He rose, tossed butt to can, and shuffled to the kitchen's mesh door. He shut it quietly and grinned at the spice rack.

Said Island Girl to English Boy

By Julia Lewis

Can I bring you back anything
from Nantucket or America?

A place?
A present?
A part?

I'll look into Nantucket Short Plays Festival.

"Could you bring California back with you,

please?

Otherwise."

"Hope you're having a great time out there, x"
x marking up the map, a piece of paper,

a promise
to California.

I'm going out
to Iowa to talk to Jim Galvin.

A poet, who wrote a whole book
about a meadow in Wyoming.

Tell me a story that will carry me back,
you came back.

"Think I'm OK."

Am I like America to you?

Greenwood

By Kimberly Nolan

she showed up
as Lily Doyle would
no plan
and unannounced

she played clawhammer
familiar
and forgotten

her travels cataloged
a roadshow circus
jerked off southern boars
slept inside Spanish rocks
farmed naked under big skies
and moved east, out of faith

in her sparkling, skintight golden suit
and rubber boots
she sings out
reverberating
through the empty rooms
of the salt marsh farmhouse

to find her
listen for the rickety bicycle
and those dancing shoes
pounding down on Jackson Square

Fatherless

By Ross Ragan

Grandpa grew up the youngest of four boys
in a turn of the century world
an Iowa farm with fresh air and green grass
and the railroad was coming to town
America was giving birth to a new age

his Papas life was shortened
and adolescent plowshares
broke new ground
the fields and the farmhouse became the classroom

He never held a diploma in his hand
yet graduated with honors
from the school of struggle and survival

visions of hope and a future
bought him a ticket on the newly laid rails
carrying him away with his burdens
to what he thought would be a better world

it wasn't long
before a pretty young girl consumed him
with goals set high
he made her a princess
on the throne of his heart
success found him out
and his kingdom was established
delivering every comfort of her heart's desire
then a baby girl, then
my dad
loved
but with an undercurrent of inconvenience

private schools and provision was made for his needs
but others did most of the child rearing

when the military called my dad's name
he shoved off
to see a very different world
and with a head full of baggage
he returned a war time hero without a parade

along came a brunette beauty ten years his younger
and worldly and wise
joined the young and wide eyed
in fatal attraction

while dad taught me to sail and lifted me into the cockpit
of fighter jets
mom broke off the tether to his world
living her life with the top down in red convertibles
every Thursday night she pulled out her hairpins
and shopped from seven to eleven
in Chanel and high heels
the grocery store was only a mile away

I watched our pantry become the spoil of promiscuity
while Dad ate from it
in voluntary denial

I was just a kid when I broke the news to him
he never recovered
and set me out to sail on a sea of forgetfulness
but another remembered me

decades later
I stood on the flight deck of an aircraft carrier
named after the father of our country
remembering my dad in sorrow for his battles lost

yet grateful for the father I came to know in his absence
my creator
staying closer to me than the air that I breathe
cheering on my victories
and lifting me out of the pits of my failures
his door is always open

so today I remain
grateful to say
that I
am not Fatherless

Forgiveness

By Trina Ragan

His turned cheek
hot from impact
though he pleads to reconcile
no compliance comes

rage emanates from her core
consuming the air
like a newly stoked fire engulfs
its surroundings

though beneath the surface
her skin is flush with shame
perception askew

she drags her feet
as to a dungeon
with unbending reluctancy to mend

but he walks slowly
and waits

patiently

knowing the reward
for the persevering
who throw aside the entanglements of struggle

anticipating enlightenment

so two can walk side by side
grace upon grace
impunity bursting forth
as peace appears
Yahuah
the One who restores

Bright Red Boots
In Loving Memory of Beth Lochtefeld

By Dan Ross

bright red boots
bright smile
bright
light
joyful ember of our being
seeking sister
of our dearest clutch
loving lover
sweet surrender
divine provender
of life sublime
happy host
joyful embrace
sweet kiss
celebrating life eternal

Jonesy

By John Stanton

We were talking about Lynn
it was the summer of learner's permits
and first dates
although it seemed every girl we knew
was already somebody's sister
our days were endless
playground basketball
and we all agreed
that over in Lynn
playing against the brothers
we would learn to be great.
or at least cool.

We talked about it
every day in June
July
half of August
we never went
it was just talk

Then one day
Jonesy pulled up
in a van
with California plates
he was the best player
we ever saw
until one day he just left
as if you could somehow just leave
the neighborhood
not for jail
or the army
those guys, anyways,
always came back
but just go.

Now, barefoot, he emerged
from the van
put up a hand
for the ball
turned in the air
a perfect jumper

None of us noticed her
until we all did
suddenly
cut off jeans
surfer girl blonde hair
sweet pot smoke rolling
out of the van
flavoring the sticky late summer air
definitely not somebody's sister
when she got bored of watching him
she simply said his name
quietly
Jonesy

He scooped up the ball
and in two dribbles
flew
lifted up
dunked with two hands
the ball hit the blacktop
spun back our way
his bare feet lightly reached
the ground

I can picture it in memory
but that day we no longer cared
they walked back to the van
she gave us a wave
tossed
her hair
smiled her Good Vibrations smile
it was the last day we ever sat around
talking about basketball
or Lynn.
fuck Lynn.
all we talked about now was
California.

Made in the USA
Charleston, SC
15 June 2014